ONE SMALL STEP

PARTICIPANT'S GUIDE

ONE SMALL STEP

PARTICIPANT'S GUIDE

THE LIFE-CHANGING ADVENTURE OF FOLLOWING GOD'S NUDGES

MATTHEW BARNETT

Chosen

a division of Baker Publishing Group
Minneapolis, Minnesota

Published by Chosen Books
11400 Hampshire Avenue South
Bloomington, Minnesota 55438
www.chosenbooks.com

Chosen Books is a division of
Baker Publishing Group, Grand Rapids, Michigan

Printed in the United States of America

ISBN 978-0-8007-9975-5

Note that in some of the author's stories, the names and identifying details of certain individuals have been changed to protect their privacy.

Cover design by Rob Williams, InsideOutCreativeArts

Author represented by The Fedd Agency, Inc.

20   21   22   23   24   25   26   7   6   5   4   3   2   1

CONTENTS

A NOTE FROM
MATTHEW BARNETT

It is always interesting to watch a baby learn to walk—the first steps are not elegant but at the same time they are beautiful. The stiff legs, the awkward movement, the eventual fall. We clap and cheer when that precious little body hits the floor because we are so elated that the little one attempted to walk in the first place. We love seeing the baby's initiative. Also, we can see the big picture, the progress toward maturity. We know that as the child grows up, he or she will reach a full range of motion and reap the benefits of these first awkward steps of courage.

Fear of moving—stagnation and complacency—can be the greatest killer of dreams. One of my goals as a pastor working with thousands of people a year who have addictions and many other life-altering issues is to show them the joy of taking that first unsteady step. I love to provoke people to do the hard thing, the thing that they know is right but that something is holding them back from doing. My belief is that whatever causes you the most resistance to taking a step forward is the thing that carries the biggest reward on the other side. Familiarity with comfort, holding a grudge, clinging to security—all must be challenged continually if you want to discover the new thing God wants to do. God is re-creating things all the time, and if we want to keep up, it is imperative to attempt to move and give Him something He can use.

For many years, I would drive home from church and eat at the fast-food restaurant Jack in the Box, always the same order: tacos and curly fries. My actions were robotic, as instinctively I would pull up and order the same unhealthy meal. One day, I saw a new salad place had opened close to my house and decided to go a different way. I broke the routine and walked in and ordered a salad. The thing that surprised me the most was that I enjoyed it. That was a turning point in my life as I went on to lose over thirty pounds. I had forgotten how good it felt to be healthy.

I am pleased that you are reading this book because I strongly believe that it will help you to become childlike again. It will give you the desire to be healthy. The goal of this book is to get us all moving again and remind us what it feels like to break free from lifeless routines and to embrace all of life's possibilities. I have so many faces in my mind as I compose this participant's guide. I am visualizing the courage of the readers of this book. I can see a tired dad and mom whose emotions have become raw from the piled-up repetition of days. Has meaning been lost in the mundane for you? I hope to help you find fresh energy for life, and I know exactly how you feel.

Have you ever been on a plane that just sat on the runway waiting for the signal to move? Most of us have. Being delayed on a runway can make us anxious, frustrated, even edgy. However, the moment the plane lifts off, we have a sense of relief that at last we are going somewhere. Let's go somewhere together through the journey of this book. For some of you, this book will challenge heart issues. Others of you will find yourself challenged to dream again and take the next step. In fact, you have already started to move simply by picking up this book. There is so much more in front of you than what is behind you. Now let's unpack what holds us back, and let's discover the possibilities of moving forward.

Open your heart to one small step!

USING THIS GUIDE

This guide is intended for you to work through as a group, a team, a youth group or even a business or a sports team. The guide goes together with the book *One Small Step*. You can get much more out of *One Small Step* by pairing it with this participant's guide and the video sessions.

This guide will explore six major discussion topics that will challenge your faith and inspire courage. I see it as a personal coaching strategy. Each of the six sessions includes the following:

- a major idea or talking point of the session
- a kick-start segment that opens the door for discussion
- notes and topics for discussion that will be explored through the questions from the video session
- questions for group discussion drawn from the Bible; my book, *One Small Step*; and day-to-day, relevant, real-life issues and experiences
- a special prayer
- a time to reflect and to strategize about your own unique path and mission going forward

In addition to the group studies, please explore the "Personal Reflection" and "Personal Action" portions at the end of each session. You may want to pursue some things on your own apart from the group, going deeper in more private and personal ways. I want this book to reach you wherever you are on your life journey.

Resources

The Scripture references throughout this guide are in the New International Version (NIV). Should you choose to use a different version, have a Bible app available to look up the verses in the translation of your choice. To get the most out of this teaching, I would also greatly encourage you to journal through digital or handwritten notes. Be sure to pick up the book, *One Small Step*, which will help you greatly with background for this study. The book will encourage you with its many stories of perseverance.

Follow the schedule below to coordinate with this participant's guide:

Read	Watch	Discuss
Introduction and chapters 1, 2 and 3 of *One Small Step*	Video session 1	Session 1, Why Not Move?
Chapter 4	Video session 2	Session 2, Rejoice in Progress
Chapters 5 and 6	Video session 3	Session 3, Little Ways to Make a Big Impact
Chapter 7	Video session 4	Session 4, Healing Others When You Need It the Most
Chapters 9, 10 and 11	Video session 5	Session 5, The Momentum of Deciding to Move
Chapters 12 and 13	Video session 6	Session 6, The Legacy of the Faithful

I am excited about taking this journey with you. Ready, set, go!

SESSION 1

Why Not Move?

Big Idea for This Session

The experiences of our lives can make us afraid to move outside of our comfort zones. Fear can bring us to our knees and rob us of a life of adventure. But when we step out in faith, our faith pleases God, and that will always bring us joy.

Session Start-Up

Have you ever noticed that one of the first words a kid will learn to say is *no*? (Have you *ever* met a kid whose first word was *yes*?) Starting out as "No" people, we grow up to become people who view limitations as a way of life. While we should not be naïve to the fact that life entails huge struggles and scary mountaintops, why do we so regularly entertain the word *no*? We use negative expressions such as, "I will never have that," or, "I can never do that." Sure, there is a chance we may fail, but is that the real issue? Could it be that the issue is not wins and losses but our fear of adventure? Could we lack the courage to go for it? We can say no for so long that we never get out of the gate to give anything a try.

Action creates possibility. The first thing that we can do to stop this cycle of never trying is to eliminate the words *no* and *never* from our vocabulary. We must stop being afraid to move. As Max Lucado says, "Meet your fears with faith." We must stop allowing fear to have unlimited access to our life. We must confront our imagined fears with hope. "Faith is confidence in what we hope for and assurance about what we do not see" (Hebrews 11:1).

Rahab heard about the God of Israel and recognized Him as the true God. The king of Jericho wanted Rahab to help him apprehend two spies, but instead she hid them and protected them (see Joshua 2). Her act of faith was so valuable that Rahab's name was included in the list of Old Testament heroes (see Hebrews 11). Hers was a classic case of taking a risk of faith, and it paid off. She had a "Why not?" attitude.

In the same way, we must fix "our eyes on Jesus, the pioneer and perfecter of faith. For the joy set before him he endured the cross, scorning its shame, and sat down at the right hand of the throne of God" (Hebrews 12:2). Notice the word *pioneer*. Also notice the phrase "the joy set before him." Joy comes through taking on challenges and exploring new attitudes and areas of growth. Every time I read that Scripture and see the word *pioneer*, I think of a New World explorer looking for gold on an expedition. Are you looking for gold? Have you made the first move to reconcile with somebody? Maybe your adventure is a call to the mission field and you have been holding back. Maybe you need to start responding in a different way in your marriage, without anger, when some problem arises. Maybe you have become resigned to bitterness.

Why not take a new step? It will be an adventure to do something out of the ordinary. Whatever is holding you back from moving, I encourage you to confront it and create a showdown between complacency and faith. Challenge the very thing that is preventing your breakthrough. Remember, "Without faith it is impossible to please God, because anyone who comes to him must believe that he exists and that he rewards those who earnestly seek him" (Hebrews 11:6).

Talk about It

If you could snap your fingers and be free from one thing instantly, what would it be? What is the one thing you would love to see happen in your life?

Video Session 1

While watching the video, use the space below to record thoughts you want to focus on.

Video Session Notes

The safest place to be is in the will of God. It is safer to take a faith-filled chance with God than to never move and play it safe.

The pros and cons do not have to line up for the idea to be a God idea. Usually, they do not. That is why it is called faith. It may feel that you are working against the odds, but God is your deliverer and He is greater than the odds.

Focus on the joy of the reward of faith more than on the cost.

Remember: God is pleased when you dream.

_____

_____

_____

_____

_____

_____

Video Discussion

1. Think about the story of buying the Queen of Angels hospital with only a few thousand dollars in church income at the time. Has there ever been a time when you needed to trust God against conventional wisdom?

2. What does radical faith look like in everyday life?

3. Have you ever wanted to attempt something out of the ordinary but fear held you back? Why?

_____

_____

_____

_____

_____

_____

Small-Group Discussion

1. The Bible is full of stories of times when people stepped
   out to do the extraordinary. The disciples saw Jesus walking on the lake. They thought it was a ghost, but Peter was
   intrigued. Peter asked Jesus if he could come out onto the
   water, too, and Jesus replied, "Come" (see Matthew 14:25–
   29). It's easy to do the ordinary thing, but when we step out
   and do something out of nature, out of character, it stretches
   our capacity. Can you remember a time where you did something against your flesh and saw the reward of faith? Did you
   feel alive?

2. Have you ever felt stopped by something from following God's
   instructions? What stopped you? Fear? Someone's opinion? A
   feeling of inadequacy? Did you overthink compassion?

3. Share about a relationship in which you were rewarded
   for moving in a direction of faith with relational change or
   reconciliation.

4. Share about a time when you took a risk to reach out to someone and they did not respond the way you thought they would.

5. Has self-doubt held you back from going after something?
   How?

6. In the first chapter of *One Small Step*, I wrote about the time
   I tried to avoid a woman addicted to drugs who showed
   up at the Dream Center. I almost missed a miracle moment because of being unwilling to go the extra mile. Can
   you remember a situation in your life where you might
   have missed an opportunity to do good? Share about it in
   your group. You might also talk about a time you did go
   out of your way to help someone and your actions made a

difference. How does stepping out into the unknown make you feel alive?

_____

_____

_____

_____

_____

_____

Bonus Questions

1. Growing up, were you surrounded by negative words? If so, how did those words shape your view about life?

2. "God anointed Jesus of Nazareth with the Holy Spirit and power, and . . . he went around doing good and healing all who were under the power of the devil, because God was with him" (Acts 10:38). Jesus had a reputation for doing good. When He was around, hungry people were fed, sick people were healed, discouraged people were uplifted. He brought change in both practical and spiritual ways. How can you and I go about building a reputation for doing good?

3. Psalm 20:4 gives us a beautiful assurance of God's love: "May he give you the desire of your heart and make all your plans succeed." Does this Scripture encourage you to believe that the best is in front of you and not behind you? Thinking about the words, "May all your plans succeed," give believing the best another try. Challenge yourself for seven days to see the

opportunity in everything. Look for hope in situations that might have appeared hopeless. Create the life God wants you to have by living on the offense rather than the defense.

Wrap-Up

Today we have learned the importance of daring to step out in faith and take a step. One small step can go a long way in changing our future. We will never know what life can be like until we undertake the first small act of courage. It might be uncertain or even scary, but it might also be the seed of a miracle. Let's take a moment and close our time in prayer. Consider these things from the discussion that you can include in your prayer:

Allow God's opinion of you to drown out every other voice.

Ask God to help you tear down the fear that has blocked you from moving in the direction of faith.

Open your heart to the nudges of the Holy Spirit as He seeks to impart ideas for how you can inspire the world around you on a regular basis.

Offer to God your willingness to find a need and fill it, and to find a hurt and heal it.

BETWEEN SESSIONS

Personal Reflection

1. Think about the times in your life when you felt the most alive, when you looked for opportunities to be a blessing to others and you were ready for the future. What changed? Do you find yourself in a lackluster place? Do you need a change of focus? Maybe, like a boxer who goes back to the old gym to try to get back to the top of his game, you need to find a way to go back to the fundamentals. Reflect on the basics: prayer, consistent reading of the Bible, the joy that comes from spiritual disciplines. Everything improves when we are in communication with God. Reflect and pray and hear the soundtrack of heaven; let Him put fire back into your soul. "I can do all this through him who gives me strength" (Philippians 4:13). With Christ, there is confidence and faith.

2. Every time you try to reestablish a prayer life, distractions will come. The enemy knows that every productive thing in your life comes from a constant relationship with God. In His presence fear diminishes and negative words fade away. Reflect below on giving control of your life back to God. Release whatever is holding you back from giving God rightful place. Let go of the baggage that holds you back by writing it down in the space below.

3. Read Proverbs 3:5–6 ("Trust in the LORD with all your heart and lean not on your own understanding; in all your ways submit to him, and he will make your paths straight.") Divide this Scripture into two parts, with the first part ending with "in all your ways submit to him" and the second part starting with "he will make your paths straight."

   In the space below see if you can create an illustration that distinguishes between God's part and our part. All we can do is love God, acknowledge Him, and let Him take us where we need to go.

   _____

   _____

   _____

   _____

   _____

   _____

   _____

Personal Action

Why not move? There is nothing to lose by trusting God in faith—and a lot to lose by holding back and playing it safe. Look for ways to serve, follow the nudge, and be willing to say yes to more ideas. Ask God to give you the power to live alert, inspired and aware of your tremendous ability to make a difference. If you are in a store and someone ahead of you is a dollar short, and you have it, pay it for them. Allow someone else to get the parking spot you wanted to have. Open the door for another person. Give your child a big hug. Ask God to give you the power to live alert, inspired and aware of your tremendous ability to make a difference. Stop rationalizing about all the reasons you cannot reach out to others. Just reach out in love because in Christ you have the capacity to do it. The world needs you to be the blessing you were created to be. Serve with courage, love with compassion and leave the day better because you have embraced the God who created it.

Prepare for The Next Session

Before you meet again, read chapter 4 of *One Small Step*.

SESSION 2

Rejoice in Progress

Big Idea for This Session

Rejoicing while you are still on the road to your destination—that is a great key to the abundant life. Victories of life ought to be celebrated more than the frustrations. If we mourn the defeats more than we celebrate the progress, we will lose the joy that God intends for us to have on the journey. Most of life is on the way to something so we might as well learn to enjoy the process. Learn to celebrate every small step of success.

Session Start-Up

Celebration keeps us going. Rejoicing in little successes paves the way to bigger victories later. Life is about building on little moments. We have the tendency to wait for the big results. *When* I have success, *then* I will celebrate. But if we do not learn to celebrate the little moments, we will never make it to celebrate the big wins. Even if you have nothing to celebrate in your own life at the moment, at least celebrate the victories of those around you. Get used to celebrating. Celebrating is the fuel station along the pathway to your future, and it is infectious. The foundation of your future is built one small victory at a time.

Resist the tendency to hold off on celebrating until you have gotten all the way to your goal. The advice to stop and smell the roses is worth remembering. Enjoy all of the little things in daily life, because they add up to big things. The psalm reminds us of the truth: "The LORD has done it this very day; let us rejoice today and be glad" (Psalm 118:24).

Many people struggling with drug addictions come through our door at the Dream Center. They have lost many things due to poor decisions. When they come into our one-year recovery program, we tell them one simple thing: Just get a little bit better every day. When you go to bed at night and you have won a battle, throw yourself a little dance party. Do it every day! Every step of progress should be celebrated. One of the greatest ways to move forward in life is to break it down into 24-hour victories. Celebrate all the way to the mountaintop even though your wins might feel microscopic along the way. As the Bible tells us, "Let us not become weary in doing good, for at the proper time we will reap a harvest if we do not give up" (Galatians 6:9).

Talk about It

Why do you think it is harder for people to make a big deal about victories than they do about defeats?

Video Session 2

While watching video session 2, use the space below to record key ideas or any thoughts you want to remember.

Video Session Notes

"Rejoice in the Lord always. I will say it again: Rejoice!" (Philippians 4:4).

The world is cynical, but we must be hopeful.

A life of rejoicing means we understand that every day brings a miracle.

We need small victories in our lives to keep us going.

There is no final arrival date with success, just a series of small wins.

There is always a reason to rejoice. Just keep looking for something, anything!

Video Discussion

1. What distractions hold you back from seeing miracles in ordinary, uneventful days?

2. Do you find yourself envious of other people's success, or do you rejoice in their progress?

3. Do you celebrate what you are becoming on the way to where you are going?

_____

_____

_____

_____

_____

_____

_____

Small-Group Discussion

1. Read the following Scriptures out loud together and discuss what God is teaching you through His Word about getting out of the cynical cycle.

   - "Since we belong to the day, let us be sober, putting on faith and love as a breastplate, and the hope of salvation as a helmet" (1 Thessalonians 5:8).

   - "Further, my brothers and sisters, rejoice in the Lord! It is no trouble for me to write the same things to you again, and it is a safeguard for you" (Philippians 3:1).

   - "I will extol the LORD at all times; his praise will always be on my lips" (Psalm 34:1).

2. When we look only to future achievements to make us happy, we lose joy in the process of getting there. Share an example of a time when you worried about an event in the future and missed the joy of daily living.

3. Share about a time in your life when someone you loved needed you but you were overly preoccupied with the affairs of your own life.

4. Can you think of a time when you did some small thing that seemed insignificant at the moment, but to someone else it was a big deal? Were you surprised by their reaction and how much it meant to them?

5. Can you think of an incident in your life when someone went out of the way to tell you something hopeful, and that became a fundamental part of positive change in your life?

6. Discuss and strategize about how you can get your childlike celebration back. What made you lose it? How can you avoid losing it again?

7. Discuss and strategize about how you can learn to decide to rejoice with someone even when you do not feel like it. How can you give when you need someone to give to you? How can you inspire other people's dreams while waiting for someone to inspire yours? What is the secret?

Bonus Questions

1. Many times, in pursuing a great goal, we get discouraged along the journey and want to quit. Gradually, the burdens of everyday life build on top one another to the point that we have a hard time seeing victory even when it is there. Psalm 34:17–19 says, "The righteous cry out, and the LORD hears them; he delivers them from all their troubles. The LORD is close to the brokenhearted and saves those who are crushed in spirit. The righteous person may have many troubles, but the LORD delivers him from them all." How can you encourage yourself when you are going through something that seems impossible to conquer?

2. Do you feel that you elevate the negatives in your life more than you do the good things? Do you grow weary under life's burdens and miss the blessings?

3. Have you ever gone to bed at night with the crushing feeling of regret, as if concrete has been poured onto you? How can you avoid regret? (Remember that whatever you do today will be your past tomorrow, and that you can change your past by making bold, positive decisions today.)

4. What are you excited about and looking forward to?

Wrap-Up

Today we have learned about the power of rejoicing in progress. My main challenge to you this: Let yourself love life. Shake free from the negative thoughts of regretting the past or wishing you were somewhere in the future. Live in the beauty of the present day. Celebrate every little victory of your life and keep moving forward. Let's close with a time of prayer together, reflecting on these things:

Thank God that His mercies are new every morning.

Ask the Holy Spirit to give you more hope for the future than regret about the past.

Pray for the discipline to learn to rejoice daily and often.

Pray for grace and mercy on behalf of others who are struggling to find joy in life, and for the strength to come alongside them to help them succeed.

BETWEEN SESSIONS

Personal Reflection

I know discouragement from the personal experience of building the Dream Center. I know how it may creep up on you. It is kind of like gray hair; one day you wake up and find your first little streak of it, and you realize that you are aging. Even giants of the faith such as King David had to contend with discouragement, depression and spiritual erosion. Read Psalm 32, in which David expresses himself about going through a tough time in his life. He recounts that his strength wasted away, and he says that he groaned all day long. What did he do about it? He simply confessed his sin. After that, the tone of the psalm shifts. Now he starts talking about the wonderful hiding place he has found in God, and he mentions singing songs of deliverance. His joy returned simply because he brought his sin before God. You are in good company when you go through a hard time, but refuse to let the enemy keep you down in the dungeon of despair. Turn to God and you will start to see a way out. Start rejoicing, even in trials. There is always something to rejoice about.

What are some things right now that you can rejoice over? Big or small, write it down below and take some time to celebrate. Just start writing below as fast as you can.

_____

_____

_____

_____

_____

_____

_____

_____

Personal Action

1. The prophet Joel said, "I will pour out my Spirit on all people. Your sons and daughters will prophesy, your old men will dream dreams, your young men will see visions. Even on my servants, both men and women, I will pour out my Spirit in those days" (Joel 2:28–29). Look deep into your heart to discover the areas of life where you have felt defined by

yesterday's failures. Visualize a big white canvas and the turning of a new page on that canvas—a new start. Create something new; let the fire of the future burn bright again. If you have confessed your sin to God, recognize that it has already been forgiven and the best way to honor God is to *believe* He forgave you and move forward. Rejoice in your salvation. Get back up and dream again. A new day is upon you, and you have a new spirit. Live like someone who has won—because you have!

2. Put some sticky notes around the house to remind yourself of the promises of God for your life. You have a glorious future ahead of you, and you can break the negative cycle with the power of the Word of God. Such notes helped me during a time of discouragement by reminding me that the power of the Word of God is bigger than my circumstances. You have victory over your past. It is time to rejoice in the present.

Prepare for the Next Session

Before you meet again, read chapters 5 and 6 of *One Small Step*.

SESSION 3

Little Ways to Make a Big Impact

Big Idea for This Session

There is no contribution too small. The miracle of our lives is found in having a game plan of service, living intentionally when it comes to doing good. Everything we do for others adds up. The legacy of our lives is found in our little acts of kindness over the years.

Session Start-Up

Years ago at the Dream Center, a lady approached me and said, "Pastor, I want to be used by God, but I have nothing to give." She had no money and no job, but she wanted to serve in some way. I told her that everyone has at least one thing they can do, and I asked her if she had a special skill. She replied that she did have one skill—the ability to design and build cardboard cars for children to play in. She could take a big, discarded cardboard box and turn it into a brightly painted Corvette or Porsche. But how could that unique talent be used for good? We came up with an idea: We would create a drive-in movie theater for all the children in the housing projects who were coming to our church. Each of them could have his or her own customized car. It was a smash hit. The little children, many of whom had never gone to a theater, arrived at the parking lot of the Dream Center, where they found their own custom-made cardboard cars in which they could sit and watch a movie. It turned out to be one of the best outreach days we have ever had in Dream Center history.

God can use anything; that's what happened when Jesus fed more than five thousand hungry people (see John 6:1–15). The crowds following Jesus were hungry and tired, and the disciples panicked when Jesus suggested that they should feed them all. Then Jesus took five barley loaves and two small fish, and He multiplied it to feed the equivalent of a whole sports arena filled with people. I love the question asked by Andrew in verse 9: "Here is a boy with five small barley loaves and two small fish, but how far will they go among so many?" Interesting question: How far will they go? The answer is quite simple. In Jesus' hands, they can go very far. Whether it is cardboard boxes on the parking lot or a little boy's lunch, God can do anything He wants with whatever we choose to give Him.

Little things make an impact. Think about how the things we re-member the most are the little things that people have done to shape our lives. We remember the teacher who took the time to love a kid who was bullied in class or the mom who shows up to record the child's sports game on her cell phone for the dad who could not make it. Those little things matter. In fact, most of what we see in the New

Testament are the personal one-on-one encounters that Jesus had with people who were dealing with ordinary problems.

There are so many ways that we can make an impact daily—if we decide to do so intentionally. I like the wording of Isaiah 32:8 in the New Living Translation: "Generous people plan to do what is generous, and they stand firm in their generosity." Generous people *plan* to be generous. In other words, their lives are guided by a strategy to be generous. Every day becomes a hunt for new ways to be a blessing. Life can be so much fun if we become intentional about doing good. We make plans for our education and careers, so why not make daily plans to be generous in some small way every day?

Talk about It

Every day when we wake up we can choose to live inwardly or outwardly. Do you have a compassion strategy?

Video Session 3

Watch video session 3. While watching this video, use the space below to record key ideas or any thoughts that spark your interest.

Video Session Notes

Live boldly, live intentionally and live to be a blessing.

Once you start to serve others, you will become addicted to making a positive difference. Look for ways to love others. Be open to what the Holy Spirit is impressing on your heart even if it feels different or uncomfortable.

Do not talk yourself out of doing good.

_____

_____

_____

_____

_____

_____

Video Discussion

1. Jesus continually challenged the disciples' view about what
   is important, bringing it down to one question: How do you
   treat other people? He said, "The greatest among you will be
   your servant. For those who exalt themselves will be humbled,
   and those who humble themselves will be exalted" (Matthew
   23:11–12). Are there certain people in your life that you find it
   harder to serve than others?

2. What is your honest view of what makes for greatness? Fame?
   Success? Or service?

3. Do you remember a time when someone said something that
   became a turning point in your life?

_____

_____

_____

_____

_____

_____

_____

_____

Small-Group Discussion

1. There are certainly some people we find easier to serve than others. Have you ever swallowed your pride (eaten humble pie) and served someone with kindness and compassion who did not deserve it? How did you feel afterward?

2. Do you find it hard to give grace to people who deserve judgment? When Jesus was dying on the cross between two others, one of the men next to him cried out for forgiveness. Jesus answered him, "Truly I tell you, today you will be with me in paradise" (Luke 23:43). Jesus gave this man freedom when he deserved judgment.

3. Can you remember a time when you did something small for someone but in that person's mind it was a big thing? Explain.

4. What holds us back from being generous? Why do you think it can be so hard to simply give people what they need?

5. Have you ever had an opportunity to be a big blessing, perhaps having the capacity to make a large donation or do something impressive. How can such an opportunity put you into a position of testing? Explain what it feels like.

6. Too often we get stuck in our inner turmoil of personal problems. What makes it hard to serve when you are carrying your own burden?

7. Brainstorm about some ways you can do good—today.

_____

_____

_____

_____

_____

_____

_____

Bonus Questions

1. In *One Small Step*, I write in chapter 5 about how it is easier to give our best when the conditions are right, but only people of character can give their best when the conditions are not favorable. I wrote, "When you put on a smile in order to make someone else's day, the world might call it hypocrisy for not being 'true to yourself.' But it is really a magnificent form of service when you would rather be served and have your ego stroked, and yet you give anyway. Selflessly, smile when you feel like frowning." How does this fit with what Jesus said in Luke 9: "Whoever wants to be my disciple must deny themselves and take up their cross daily and follow me" (verse 23)?

2. Do you find it easier to be kinder to people who have committed sins that do not offend you as much as others? How is your pride involved in this?

3. Speculate about what it would be like to walk into a room thinking, *How can I brighten someone else's day?*

Wrap-Up

Today, we have learned that generosity can be a way of life, that we can listen to the Holy Spirit to show us ways we can make a difference, and that a servant of Christ finds joy in being obedient one step at a time. We have also explored what true biblical greatness is. The world tells us to ascend to greatness by climbing the ladder, but God wants us to hold the ladder so that others may climb up. Success is not a far-off goal because it comes right now when you serve those around you, wherever you are. Success is easy to achieve, because it simply means being a servant. Here are some things to pray about:

Ask God to give you a heavenly perspective about success.

Confess that at times you have missed little moments to make a difference.

Commit to a life of speaking only edifying words.

Ask God to give you a daily strategy for generous living.

BETWEEN SESSIONS

Personal Reflection

1. You can choose to live aware of the needs of others, to stay responsive, fresh and alive to the plight of other people. You can choose not to give up on people. "But as for you, be strong and do not give up, for your work will be rewarded" (2 Chronicles 15:7). Declare:

   - "I don't have to serve, I get to serve!"
   - "I bring value to the world around me, and I have something to give a broken world."
   - "There is no seed that's too small when it comes to helping others."
   - "I have the power to bring life to everyday situations, and I'm going to be a blessing. I have something to give the world, and I will not let fear hold me back from being generous." "For the Spirit God gave us does not make us timid, but gives us power, love and self-discipline" (2 Timothy 1:7).
   - "I will leave a legacy of kindness and compassion. I am deciding to walk forward with a disposition of service to the world around me."

2. Memorize as many Scriptures as you can that deal with being generous and serving others. By doing so, you will be reminded of the promise of blessing that comes to those who serve.

3. Kindness is something we must work on in the current environment of destructive social media in which skepticism and cynicism become too easy. Ask the Holy Spirit to keep your heart tender and to help you avoid being lured into the trap of meaningless battles or anything that counters the spirit of love

and forgiveness. Determine to be a bridge builder. What are some of the traps you face that can lure you into negativity?

Personal Action

Decide to spend five minutes a day for the next thirty days intentionally making a difference. Whether it is a thoughtfully written text message, a kind phone call or any act of compassion, just get in the habit of thinking outward and being a blessing. Praise your spouse. Restrain yourself from reacting out of frustration. Ask the Holy Spirit to reveal to you what you can do; follow His nudges. Start listening to the voice that opposes what your flesh wants.

Prepare for the Next Session

Before the group meets again, read chapters 7 and 8 in *One Small Step*.

SESSION 4

Healing Others
When You Need It the Most

Big Idea for This Session

Serving others can help you heal yourself. You do not have to have it all together to be used by God. Your burden is someone else's blessing.

Session Start-Up

I have met many people over the years who have said the same thing to me: "I will get involved in ministry when I get it all together." Yet none of us will ever find ourselves in a perfect situation—and that is the point. God uses us anyway. It is like saying, "When everything is perfect, then I'll come to church."

God can use you anytime. If you are struggling under a burden, you can serve out of that burden. Jesus said, "Come to me, all you who are weary and burdened, and I will give you rest. Take my yoke upon you and learn from me, for I am gentle and humble in heart, and you will find rest for your souls. For my yoke is easy and my burden is light" (Matthew 11:28–30). The burden of the Lord is easy because it is a burden of giving. The load is light because you are emptying yourself rather than adding baggage along the way.

When you need to be served, the best thing you can do is go out and serve someone else. The enemy loves to keep you in isolation where he can speak to you about your insufficiency. But you can serve regardless of your difficulties. You always have something to give, and God can use even your own hard time to benefit another person. Keep serving in every season of your life, whether you feel qualified or not. It is always worth it.

When you need healing, put yourself into someone else's world. Reach out with what you have, and it will bring you the healing you need. One day, a lady who was struggling with depression came to my office. I am not the world's best counselor, but I do know the healing power of serving. I wrote her a note that looked like a doctor's prescription:

Day 1: Go to the Dream Center and help feed the hungry.

Day 2: Volunteer in the kitchen.

Day 3: Spend time writing letters to prison inmates.

Day 4: Go out with Dream Center crew and clean the streets.

I wrote down an entire week of things to do, and she did them. The next week, I sent her off with another list. The next week, she missed our meeting, and again the following week. I saw her in church and asked, "Why didn't you show up?" She told me she had been so busy serving other people, making meals and reaching out, that she had forgotten about her depression. That is how it works! It is possible to serve your way out of your struggle.

Talk about It

Have you ever felt unqualified to do something for God?

Video Session 4

Watch Video session 4. While viewing the video, use the space below to record key ideas or any thoughts you want to remember.

Video Session Notes

There is a way to lighten the burden of life.

You will never be worthy, so do not wait until everything is perfect to make a difference. Jesus qualified you for God's service when He gave His life for you; you cannot earn the right to be useful by your own efforts.

Your greatest regret can become your greatest weapon.

You are valuable and useful no matter what you've gone through. The world needs you to step out and be real.

What do you have left? Present it to God for His service. Regardless of what it is, it will be enough, and it is a treasure.

Video Discussion

1. How have you downplayed the value of your life and what you can contribute to others?

2. Can someone be disqualified from serving by sin or foolishness?

3. Scripture tells us that Samson's greatest victory came at the end of his life when he killed more Philistines than he ever had before (see Judges 16). Do you believe that God can restore someone from complete failure and bring them back to even greater usefulness?

Small-Group Discussion

1. How do we sometimes count people out because of their past failures?

2. How can the Church extend more grace in restoring people back to usefulness?

3. Discuss how certain sins such as adultery, drug addiction or fornication affect a person's usefulness to God's work afterward. Do you believe that God can take those sins and redeem them into something even more powerful than if the sins had never been committed? If so, share examples.

4. In chapter 8 of *One Small Step*, I describe a season in my life when I felt lifeless in the ministry. I felt drained by people's needs. After preaching on Sunday mornings, I just went home and did not want to talk to anyone. I realized quickly that I had run from the basics of fellowship with Christ. I had failed to pursue the fundamental thing: communion with God through prayer. Have you ever gone without praying or seeking God for a time? What changed about your life during that time? What made you come back to a life of prayer and devotion to God, and how did that help?

5. In chapter 7 of *One Small Step*, I write: "The darkest place I have ever lived is in the place of comparison, worrying about where I am versus where I want to be." Discuss what this statement has meant in your own life. How have you gotten off track by trying to live someone else's life instead of flourishing in your own calling?

6. If you can, describe a time when you left your personal pity party to go and meet someone else's need. Did you go back to your pity party afterward? How did reaching out to others change your outlook?

Bonus Questions

1. Scripture urges you to "humble yourselves, therefore, under God's mighty hand, that he may lift you up in due time. Cast all your anxiety on him because he cares for you" (1 Peter 5:6–7). How does humbling yourself bring reward from God?

2. What is one thing in your life you would love to see God restore?

_____

_____

_____

_____

_____

_____

Wrap-Up

Today, we have learned that it is never too late for God to use anyone. The only thing holding us back from being useful is the lies of the enemy. The enemy wants to paralyze action; he wants us to believe that we are "less than." But God has a special place in His heart for anyone who wants to make a comeback. We have also learned that living outward can heal much of what we may be dealing with on the inside. Jesus said, "Give, and it will be given to you. A good measure, pressed down, shaken together and running over, will be poured into your lap. For with the measure you use, it will be measured to you"

(Luke 6:38). When we give goodness we get the "bounce back" effect of faith. Let's believe these things together in prayer:

Ask for faith to believe that more mountains are still out there to climb.

Ask God to help you find someone to serve even when you may need to be served.

Thank God that He is never done with you and that He can use you regardless of your qualifications.

Ask God for the faith to dream again.

BETWEEN SESSIONS

Personal Reflection

1. No matter what you may be going through, stop and think about someone you know who is going through a hard time. Put aside the burdens that you are carrying and try your best to feel that person's burden. Write down a few prayers for that person and ask the Holy Spirit to show you ways, even unconventional ways, that you can reach out. Do not be afraid to step out of your comfort zone. Write down some ideas for how you can be a blessing to this person.

2. Proverbs 24:16 says, "Though the righteous fall seven times, they rise again, but the wicked stumble when calamity strikes." You may have fallen in some way because of the actions of others, brokenness or your own mistakes. Start thinking about getting back up, even if you feel that you are too far down to do it. Below, write in faith how incredible your

comeback will be. Speak life into your future. On the blank canvas before you, paint a picture with words about the new person that God is raising up. Dare to dream again!

_____

_____

_____

_____

_____

_____

Personal Action

There is power in our words.

1. Get started! Just start speaking life into your future. Moving forward by speaking life into your dreams. Tell the others in your group, "Something new is happening in me. I'm going to use whatever I have to serve others." Let the people around you see your confidence. Come out of your shell, and use everything that you have experienced to bring life to someone else. See your burden in a new light and serve out of your place of struggle. Serve with whatever measure of influence that you have to lift the burdens of others. You will not have to look far to find a need—needs are everywhere!

2. Realize that God has covered you with His full armor (see Ephesians 6:10–17) only so that you can move forward. You do not have a breastplate or shield on your backside, so you must forget about your past. God has armed you to move ahead and advance.

3. Start with your own family. Build up the people closest to you. Get in the habit of speaking encouragement to those who are most familiar to you and with whom you interact the most. Let them benefit from the abundance of your heart. Look for times when they feel the most discouraged. Serve the ones you love with words of love. Remember that you cannot truly express your love for others until you have felt the freeing love of Christ.

4. Be a need hunter, the kind of person who listens to the whispers of the needs around you, and who responds with compassion. Ask God to give you an ear that hears what others are going through.

5. Let every morning remind you of second chances and new beginnings. The level of your usefulness rises in response to your level of surrender. It has never been about what you have done in the past, it is what you have chosen to be right now. Go for it!

You can be sure that the sun will come up in the morning. In the same way, life starts all over again. Get up and take one small step toward others. Someone needs your joy, your compassion, your struggle, your strength.

Prepare for the Next Session

Before the group meets again, read chapters 9, 10 and 11 of *One Small Step*.

SESSION 5

The Momentum
of Deciding to Move

Big Idea for This Session

It is not easy to leave your personal comfort zone and to reach for new horizons. The only way to experience an extraordinary future is to take that first step in the direction of the unknown.

Session Start-Up

You never know what is possible until you take the first step toward the unknown. I will never forget the day I was taking a casual jog around the Rose Bowl in Pasadena when a man sent me a text saying, "Pastor, you should run the World Marathon Challenge." He sent me the link about it, and when I read it, I was shocked. The challenge was to run seven marathons on seven continents on *seven consecutive days*—a full marathon (26.2 miles) on every continent of the world (including Antarctica), all within 168 hours. He sent a follow-up text suggesting it could be a fundraiser for the Dream Center and pledging $100,000 himself. We were in great financial difficulty, but there was no way I could meet such a challenge. Realizing, however, that I could not turn my back on that kind of donation, I responded with a reluctant yes, and I undertook the overwhelming training process. I was training for the impossible. In chapters 2 and 3 in *One Small Step*, I talk in detail about the whole experience.

This experience taught me many things, but the main lesson was that everything becomes more possible when you simply start walking toward a goal. I did finish the World Marathon Challenge against all odds, but really the victory was won before the race. It came through that initial decision to take the first step.

Momentum is a powerful thing; it means that one small act of faith can go a long way. Like a magnet, momentum attracts and pulls even greater momentum toward itself. People are drawn toward momentum. Families flourish in momentum.

Paul talks about living in this place of God's appointment. "We do not dare to classify or compare ourselves with some who commend themselves. When they measure themselves by themselves and compare themselves with themselves, they are not wise. We, however, will not boast beyond proper limits, but will confine our boasting to the sphere of service God himself has assigned to us, a sphere that also includes you. We are not going too far in our boasting, as would be the case if we had not come to you, for we did get as far as you with the gospel of Christ" (2 Corinthians 10:12–14). When you are in the place to which God has appointed you, momentum flourishes.

Block out distractions, listen to the Holy Spirit as He tells you who you are in Christ, resist the temptation to compare yourself to others, and start taking steps that build momentum. Take the first hard step, explore the unknown, and watch momentum begin to take over. Do not let fear hold you back as you get used to saying yes to the call of Christ.

Talk about It

Why is it so hard to break free from the pressures and ordinary flow of life?

Video Session 5

Watch video session 5. While watching the video, use the space below to record any key ideas or thoughts you want to remember.

Video Session Notes

The miracle space is what you can do versus what you cannot do. Create a distance between what you can do and what you cannot do, and give God room to work. He will help you do the impossible, and He gets the glory.

God loves it when we trust Him enough to take a step of faith.

God has miracles along the way that you cannot see until you move forward. We must be in motion to find out what those miracles are.

Remember that "without faith it is impossible to please God, because anyone who comes to him must believe that he exists and that he rewards those who earnestly seek him" (Hebrews 11:6). Faith is the currency of heaven. God loves it when we step out into our uncomfortable zones because it shows that we love Him enough to trust Him to deliver us.

_____

_____

_____

_____

_____

Video Discussion

1. How can you create a miracle space for God to work through you? Why do most of us prefer to stay in our comfort zones instead of stepping up to new challenges?

2. When you challenge aspects of your life where you have conceded ground for years (certain belief systems, attitudes, lack of courage) how does it make you feel? Scared? Alive?

3. What does it mean to be "born on the 50-yard line"? How might someone born with major disadvantages naturally develop a stronger faith than someone who was raised with many advantages?

_____

_____

_____

_____

Small-Group Discussion

1. In chapter 9 of *One Small Step*, I tell the story about a home-less man with no shoes who entered our recovery home at the Dream Center. It was hard to find shoes for this man because he wore a size 20. A man in our church had a contact with a team member of the Dodgers, so he sent him a text message. The result was that one of the team members who wore size 20 shoes not only presented the man with a collection of shoes but also invited him to Dodger stadium and gave him the royal treatment. Everything started from one simple step—a text message. Discuss how small steps really matter. See if you can think of personal examples from your own lives.

2. Do you regret an opportunity that you had to make a differ-ence but fear overcame the possibility of a miracle? Even if we miss opportunities to do good God will give us another oppor-tunity. What will you do next time?

3. What happens when momentum is going in the wrong direc-tion? Often in sports when the opposing team gets ahead, the other team calls a time-out to turn things around. The time-out removes them from the crisis of the game and helps them regroup. How is this like going back to the disciplines of prayer and reading the Word of God when we seem to be los-ing ground in life?

4. One of the verses that most challenges my compassion on a day-to-day level is Proverbs 3:27–28, which reads. "Do not withhold good from those to whom it is due, when it is in your power to act. Do not say to your neighbor, 'Come back tomorrow and I'll give it to you'—when you already have it with you." What holds you back from doing good when you have the power to do it? How can you overcome your tendency to hold back?

5. In chapter 11 of *One Small Step*, I talk about taking risks. The idea of taking risks on people in trouble is dear to my heart. It is difficult because we would prefer to serve people who deserve it. Have you ever taken a risk on someone who hurt you, causing you to be reluctant to help a troubled soul again? Have you taken a risk on someone others have given up on, and it became a turning point?

6. Also in chapter 11 of *One Small Step*, I talk about an elderly homeless man in our church that we call Dancing Lloyd. Dancing Lloyd is relentless in giving praise to God. He is a walking dance party. His life of unrestrained praise is a lesson on the simplicity of enjoying the simple truth that we have a relationship with our Creator. How is this different from living life for the applause of others? What does it mean to live for an audience of One?

Bonus Questions

1. What are some things you can do to get your momentum going back in the right direction?

2. When Jesus was dying on the cross even those close to him thought it was over. They felt that His death was the end of an era. The truth was that through His death Jesus was about to bring life. Many times we pray that God will fill us up, but sometimes He dries us up to expose things about our life that we need to see. What needs to dry up and be exposed in your life in order to experience momentum in your future?

_____

_____

_____

_____

_____

_____

Wrap-Up

The hardest step to take is the first one. Have you ever noticed that when you decide to start praying again or reading the Bible again, every possible distraction suddenly arises? The enemy does not like our first steps in the right direction because he knows they will lead to more. Isaiah put it in a unique way: "A bruised reed he will not break, and a smoldering wick he will not snuff out" (Isaiah 42:3). This Scripture inspires me, because it tells me that as long as there is a little smoke left there's still a chance for a fire. Momentum can begin when there is just a little smoke left. In fact, you can consider the distractions and obstacles a *confirmation* to take the first step. Your call has value, and that is why your first step of courage is under attack. As you pray about these things, let courage arise!

Thank the Lord for the trials of your past.

Thank God that He makes usefulness out of brokenness and
that you can dream again.

Thank the Lord for helping you feel the fire once again and to
step out in faith.

BETWEEN SESSIONS

Personal Reflection

I remember holding the hand of a man in our rehab program as he
went through a horrible drug withdrawal. It was brutal to watch. It
seemed hopeless; everything inside of him wanted to go back to the
heroin needle. I cannot put into words the nightmarish torture he
was going through. Not only was he dealing with the physical mani-
festations of the struggle to get clean, but his mind was tormented
by a demonic presence. I felt helpless. The only thing I could say that
seemed to help this tortured man was, "Keep going. There is something beyond your pain." My encouragement was not perfect, but it
was enough to keep him in the bed, going through the process. Even-
tually his head became clear, and he moved forward into his future
in the Kingdom of God. He kept surviving day-to-day long enough
to see his miracle. His step of momentum meant not moving at all
but rather just lying there. He had to recover before he could really
move. It is always a beautiful thing to see life return, step-by-step, to
someone who is broken.

Momentum comes in different ways. For one person, it might be
breaking the cycle of negativity by deciding to pray again. For others,
it might mean loving the ones who have hurt them the most. Often

it can come in the form of giving to someone who has a need when you have a need of your own. God can use any expression of faith. He loves you so much that He is quick to take any forward movement and turn it into a wave of momentum by which He can bless you and others. Offer God your seed of faith. He will smile from heaven and say, "I can work with that."

Take a few minutes to speak to your loving Father in heaven about your next move of faith. Never fear that it will be too small or insignificant, because it will be the beginning of something new.

_____

_____

_____

_____

_____

_____

_____

_____

Personal Action

Give God a baby step. Start a new discipline that you've been lacking. Don't let life live you; start living it.

Prepare for the Next Session

Before we meet again, Read chapters 12 and 13 of *One Small Step*.

SESSION 6

The Legacy
of the Faithful

Big Idea for This Session

Leaving a legacy will always be more about who you are rather than what you do. A person's character outlives performance and accomplishments. Life accomplishments will fade, but who you are will live forever.

Session Start-Up

Jesus accomplished a lot on this earth. He healed the sick, cast out demons and drew crowds to hear Him preach. He ministered to the masses, and although His ministry reached a much smaller number of people than many churches do today, two thousand years later, countless people all over the world still read about their incredible Savior, Jesus Christ, and they follow Him passionately. Christians today may accomplish notable things, but Jesus is the one who set everything in motion. In an unparalleled way, He showed people a new way of living. He bequeathed true salvation to anyone who would follow Him, and His perfectly virtuous character is the reason people want to follow Him. They do not follow Him and talk about Him because of long-ago good deeds, but because of His blamelessness, his merit—that is what lives on as His legacy.

The parable in the talents is a great picture of the legacy of faithfulness. Matthew 25 tells the story of a master who went on a journey and entrusted three of his servants to manage his wealth at home. Before he departed, the master left bags of gold in his servants' safekeeping, giving the first servant five bags of gold, another two bags, and a third servant one bag, hoping to see his enterprise expand in his absence (see verses 14–18). The first servant doubled the wealth and so did the second one. But the man who had received one bag of gold hid his master's money in a hole in the ground to protect it from thieves. Upon his return much later, the master was quite pleased with the first two servants, but so angry with the third that he commanded, "Take the bag of gold from him and give it to the one who has ten bags" (Matthew 25:28).

Notice that the master gave the same praise to each of the first two servants, although they had started and finished with different amounts of money. Both were called faithful. But the third servant had been too fearful to do anything, and he ended up with nothing.

Greatness in the Kingdom of God depends on what you do with whatever starting point you have been presented with in life. I have known many people who, through faithfulness and determination, have overcome early years of neglect, heartache and pain to find Christ and flourish. They leave a legacy of what it means to know Jesus as their Savior.

What inspires people more than how much you have accomplished is how far you have come from wherever you started. One day I made a crazy statement in church, saying, "The best Christian in this room might be a smoker!" The audience looked at me funny. I explained: "This person might have been raised with no knowledge of Christ, been beaten every day by his father and had no support of a loving church. He has come a long way. So what if he still has this one last problem of smoking? I contrast him with the person who was raised by great parents who took him to church and who blessed him with every resource. He has lived his entire life without committing any of the "major" sins. But even with that great foundation, he has never stretched himself. Instead, he has buried his gifts and has never made a difference for Christ."

How far will you take what has been given to you? Spiritual growth is vital to leaving a legacy, and what you choose to do with what you have is what will inspire the generations to come.

Talk about It

What kind of legacy of spiritual growth would you like to leave? What character quality would you most like to be remembered by?

Video Session 6

Watch video 6. While viewing the video, use the space below to record key ideas or any thoughts you want to remember.

Video Session Notes

Stay hungry all the time.

Never take shortcuts to the promises God has for you.

The little things you do tell the story of your life. They are the things that often people remember the most.

What you overcome might just be your legacy.

It is never too late to change unhealthy patterns.

_____

_____

_____

_____

_____

_____

Video Discussion

1. Have you ever been caught in the trap of comparing your talents with someone else's? What makes this so tempting? Why is it unhelpful?

2. Can you identify the primary spiritual battle that is blocking you from moving forward and leaving a legacy? How are you dealing with it?

3. Is it ever too late to leave a positive legacy? Why or why not?

_____

_____

_____

_____

_____

_____

Small-Group Discussion

1. Name a positive quality that others have said you have that you might have buried instead of investing it toward others.

2. Can you think of a reason why you might have buried your gift? Perhaps it was words spoken to you as a child or a difficult event. Read God's promise in Isaiah 41:13: "For I am the LORD your God who takes hold of your right hand and says to you, Do not fear; I will help you."

3. In chapter 13 of *One Small Step*, I talk about leaving a local legacy by doing a lot of small things with great faithfulness. What are some small things you can do right now to start a new pattern of doing good works?

4. Proverbs 20:7 says, "The righteous lead blameless lives; blessed are their children after them." Have you spent much time thinking about the things you want to be remembered for?

5. When people in our recovery program overcome shame, they can move forward and grow. Their restoration is sometimes so remarkable that I have had to pinch myself to believe it. Share about how shame may have affected your own life.

6. In chapter 12 of *One Small Step*, I tell the story of a man who was hiding in a garbage can from the police when a lady told him to go to the Dream Center and change his life. He is now a hero around our campus because he bounced back up from rock bottom. Do you know someone who is on rock bottom who could use a little love and encouragement from you?

7. One thing I have learned from my father (82 years old at this writing) is that you are never too old to grow. He constantly tells me, "I need to work on this." Could it be that one of the legacies he is leaving is the desire to keep growing and the perseverance to keep trying to improve? Discuss areas where you think you can challenge complacency in yourself, where you have settled for less than you should have.

Bonus Questions

1. In chapter 13 of *One Small Step*, I talk about everyone having a superpower. The Incredible Hulk has strength, Superman has invincibility and Batman has cool gadgets. What is your great quality?

2. Since you have been reading this participant's guide, what are some ways you have started to move forward with?

3. What small steps do you feel liberated to take in moving forward with your life? Do you feel inspired to dream again or to move in a direction in which you have lacked faith?

_____

_____

_____

_____

_____

_____

_____

_____

Wrap-Up

My desire is for you to be motivated to move forward, and with God's help to leave a good legacy. I know from experience that it is never too late to get up and go; the Bible is about imperfect people leaving a legacy. God can take whatever you have left and turn it into a miracle. The fact that you have read this guide and engaged in this study is proof that there is something in you that is ready for more. Are you starting to explore the extent of what you can be in Christ? Let's wrap up our time together in prayer. You might want to consider these things:

Ask God to give you a sudden breakthrough. (It is a bold prayer, but God still does instant miracles.)

Repent of the attitude of feeling that your life is defined by your past.

Thank God for the capacity to hunger and thirst for righteousness.

Ask God to multiply the influence He has given you so that you can leave a legacy.

In prayer, determine never to bury your talent, through God's help.

Give Him praise in advance for the victories you are about to win.

AFTER THE SESSION

Personal Reflection

This participant's guide has come to an end, but a glorious new start awaits you. God is giving you the power to move in freedom toward your future. He can use even your past mistakes for His glory. God wants you to step toward your future. Give Him something to work with, and He will bless it. The Dream Center ministry started with a desk on the sidewalk with three bags of food. It was not much, but it was the first step. Years later, God honored that first step and gave us a hospital. The seed you present to God is crucial, a test of the intentions of your heart and an expression of your faith. It is valuable, and it is enough in God's hand.

Remember the following truths:

- You have nothing to fear when the purpose for your life is in God's hands. "The LORD is my light and my salvation—whom shall I fear? The LORD is the stronghold of my life—of whom shall I be afraid?" (Psalm 27:1).

- Take a step and watch God move. "Now he who supplies seed to the sower and bread for food will also supply and increase your store of seed and will enlarge the harvest of your righteousness" (2 Corinthians 9:10).

- Live in awe and wonder. "Who among the gods is like you, Lord? Who is like you—majestic in holiness, awesome in glory, working wonders?" (Exodus 15:11).

- Any step forward is just fine. Jesus said to an invalid man by the pool of Bethesda: "Get up! Pick up your mat and walk" (John 5:8). The man had remained in the same situation for 38 years before Jesus told him to rise. God can turn things around even after years of stagnation. I encourage you to read this entire story in John 5:1–18 to understand the significance of this sudden turnaround and the magnitude of the resulting miracle.

- Tune out every voice of the past and listen to the Holy Spirit nudging you into a life of confidence and courage. Make these words your own: "I can do all this through him who gives me strength" (Philippians 4:13). It does not depend upon your strength, but His!

Personal Action

This book has been written from the perspective of someone who has seen God do anything. I have seen infamous gang members bow before Christ, and I have seen fallen pastors restored. I have seen judges sentence people to the Dream Center instead of giving them a 25-year prison sentence.

If I could reach through the pages of this book and give you a big hug, I would. I tell you truthfully that you are going to make it, because with God's help, you are! Whatever you do, do not just stand still. Do not allow yourself to get stuck in regret. Instead, love out of your deepest regret, serve out of your greatest failure and take the stick with which the enemy is beating you out of his hand—so that you can use it against him. What do you want God to restore? Write it down, present it to Him and stop worrying about how you are going to recover what you have lost. Focus on getting back your relationship with God.

That is the one great takeaway. If you have a relationship with God, then you have everything. Jesus said, "Seek first his kingdom and his righteousness, and all these things will be given to you as well" (Matthew 6:33). I love how Jesus refers to even the major concerns of our lives as simply "things." The main reason I tell you to write down the things you want restored is so that you can mark them off one by one when God takes care of them. Just write down those things that you need, and trust God to take care of them—and then focus on taking steps toward spiritual growth. Start praying, start reading the Word of God, start stepping toward needy people.

In closing, after you have written the list of things you want God to restore, create a list of personal declarations such as this:

I am never going to look back.

I am going to celebrate victories and not condemn myself in defeat.

I am going to celebrate every step of progress.

I am going to get up quickly when I fall.

I am going to love everyone, even those who do not deserve it.

I am going to serve even when I need to be served myself.

I am going to take a risk on loving risky people.

I am going to leave a legacy of godliness to my children.

Just step out and start to move. I can't wait to see what will happen! I love you, I am proud of you and I am always here for you.

Matthew Barnett is senior pastor of the historic Angelus Temple and the Dream Center in Los Angeles, California, now one of over 150 Dream Centers around the world. He and his father, megachurch pastor Tommy Barnett, co-founded the L.A. Dream Center under the auspices of the Assemblies of God in 1994. In 2001, the Dream Center was formally united with Angelus Temple, the flagship Foursquare church founded by Aimee Semple McPherson. A congregation over 7,000 now attends weekly, and the Dream Center reaches more than 30,000 people weekly with its needs-based ministries and outreaches.

Matthew is in demand across the country as a speaker for churches, conferences and camp meetings, and, with George Barna, is the author of the bestselling book, *The Cause within You*. His other books include *The Church that Never Sleeps* and *Misfits Welcome*.

Matthew and his wife, Caroline, have a daughter and a son, and they make their home in the Los Angeles area.

—**Visit**—
matthewbarnett.com
dreamcenter.org
thedcnetwork.org
angelustemple.org

ADDITIONAL NOTES

Additional Notes

Additional Notes